Books

Gird yourselves:

for ye shall be broken in pieces

it shall come to pass

Behold the light of despair

the glare of anguish

and ye shall be driven to darkness

If there is blasting

    (there shall be blasting)

the names of offenders shall be shouted from the rooftops

Sarah Kane

4.48 Psychosis

Quasar Love

A Reenactment in Three Acts

by Anton Bonnici

Foreword

by Genna Rivieccio

Contents

Foreword

If you were looking for a play about love in the "Taylor Swift spirit of things," you've come to the wrong place (and not just because Tay never wrote a song about having the shit smacked out of her by one of her boyfriends or wanting to stare into a person's many bodily holes). Close this book and walk away from it right now before you enter a void from which you cannot return. And yes, *Quasar Love* is all about voids. Or rather, the black hole that love both causes and leaves in its wake. "Where does 'everything' start?" Terry asks on more than one occasion in the play. "With explosions, explosions in space, stars die, and explode in space, and when stars die, they leave giant holes behind them, and these giant holes sometimes become special, very special. The most special thing in the universe. The greatest thing in the universe. Quasars."

Terry goes on to explain the unique nature of quasars, how they have "an amazing paradoxical feature; the supermassive black hole pulls in dust and matter at such speeds that the debris forms a spinning disc of breaking matter just before it all gets sucked into its vortex." The parallel to *l'amour* itself isn't hard to see, with Terry continuing, "The disc of spinning matter heats up enough to shoot out an unfathomable jet of radioactive light, a steady and unstoppable stream of light capable of breaking through its own galaxy and traveling across the universe for millions of lightyears, across space and time itself, straight into our very eyes… Light shooting out of the darkness." Apart from the highly evocative-of-ejaculation imagery, this description, too, is meant to serve as a mirror of love's own miraculousness. Of being able to tap into that rare moment that would actually bring someone to you from across space and time so that you both could exist exactly in this moment to be together. To "find" each other. And then likely destroy each other soon after.

That quasar explosion in the galaxy is something like *la petite mort*. The "little death" doesn't only signify orgasm in French. Its meaning can extend to love being its own kind of death via the self-sacrifice that tends to come with it. And, even though one shouldn't automatically equate sex with love, the two so often become inextricably linked. Yet sex and (/or) love never seem to be truly enough, not to fill that big black hole within all of us. One that Jennifer tries to stop up with her quest for fame of some sort. *Recognition* of her talents— this is a play about the true artist's suffering as much as it is about love. About society's timeless need to make redundant those who don't fit into it. Because, sadly, it is never ourselves we look to for validation, but always the outside world. The so-called "tastemakers" who decide which people will be "plugged" and which will remain in the proverbial slush pile.

While *Quasar Love* addresses the "two against the world" quality that can so often bring a couple (particularly an artistic couple) together, it does not present love with rose-colored glasses by any stretch (here Terry would think of a woman's ass cheeks being pulled apart). In dichotomous fashion, it is as much anti-love as it is "pro"-love. As Jennifer asks, "How could such a duality take shape in the same celestial object?" It's a question that also extends to the notion that man and woman together present a duality (not to get all heteronormative on you). The yin and the yang. Both complementing each other *and* being totally at odds. It's why Terry's viciousness when it comes to his sexual urges can never be realized by Jennifer. Why Jennifer's own sexual desires can never adequately be fulfilled by Terry. And sex itself isn't enough anyway, "a pathetic bodily function," Jennifer calls it, adding, "We can't close the holes inside our beings with some sweaty biological exercise that's only a few measures away from the pleasures of eating and defecating."

In the end, they must blow everything to pieces, body and all. For none of us can go on existing if we actually expect to be satisfied. Least of all by the construct of love that has been part of a centuries-long marketing campaign in literature of every variety. Not, however, in *Quasar Love*. No, this work seeks to drop an atom bomb on every stupid human paradigm and ask that we start over again, or maybe not bother to recommence at all the broken cycle of love—wherein one person's gravitational pull sucks in another. Until both are reduced to space dust.

Genna Rivieccio

Editor, The Opiate Books

Play Notes

The events referred to in this play take place in a metropolitan city at some point in the mid-1990s. This is a work of fiction. All characters and events are fictional and any resemblance to real life people or situations is purely coincidental.

Characters:

Terry – a young man in his twenties

Jennifer – a young woman in her thirties

Journalist – a person in their forties

Young woman – a traumatized teenager

Theatre Owner – a man in his fifties

Survivor – a person in their forties

Brother – a man in his forties

Psychologist – a person in their forties

Critic – a person in their fifties

Sergeant – a man in his forties

Actors – the actors playing Jennifer and Terry

Set:

A small studio apartment with a double bed and a kitchen corner. A lot of notebooks are strewn across the floor. Next to the bed there is a chair with clothes on it. Exit right leads to an unseen small shower and toilet. A door can be seen upstage back left. The door remains closed.

Projections:

Pornography—throughout the performance, there are pornographic projections that are meant to be shown on top of the action on stage. The depictions should not be realistic but rather surreal or cartoonish.

Cosmic Images—unlike the pornography, these images should contain strong, vivid detail with colour and complexity.

Interviews—the interviews should be projected on a separate screen away from the action onstage.

N.B.: / means the next line overlaps here.

Act One

00

ONSCREEN

A city—loud noises of traffic, construction, people talking, sounds of chaotic life. Lots of neon signs and lights and posters; giant posters with famous stars everywhere. Then an ambulance, sirens; we come to a theatre with red tape, the place is clearly quarantined, police are everywhere, two or three ambulances are also onsite. A small crowd is gathered to look at what is happening. Someone is crying. Stretchers with black body bags are being brought out of the theatre and loaded into vans.

FADE TO BLACK

01

ONSTAGE

TERRY is on the floor of a studio apartment. Notebooks litter the floor everywhere. TERRY is writing in a notebook and talks as he writes.

NOTE: TERRY is writing and reading from his notebooks all throughout the play. At times he might be writing as he speaks, like he's dictating to himself, other moments he might be re-reading from a notebook and rewriting, sometimes he's musing off-book before returning to the notes. This behaviour is not always explained in the directions, the actor playing TERRY may play

TERRY: I'm a great writer she said, I can do it she said. I can write something amazing for her. So, I'm going to. I'm going to write for her, not just something, but "everything." That's exactly what I'm going to do. She wants me to write for her, so I'll write for her. And I'll start right here.

This is me deciding to write everything down. This is me, writing down my decision to write everything down.

And I'm saying it out loud. I'm saying it out loud as I'm writing it down. There. This is going to be easy.

Writing and reading. That's all it is. Write everything. Read everything. Life. All of it. For her. I will write it and read it, all for her.

(Pause. Thinking. Sudden drop in enthusiasm.)

Where do I start? Where does "everything" start?

With a bang, everything started with an explosion, violence. Then there was a hole. A black hole that needed to be filled; a wound that needed to be sutured. That is life. Life is when a wound tries to heal itself.

What if we are wounds in space and time forever pulsing between pain and solace?

But black holes never find solace, they devour forever, and once they're done devouring they're no longer black holes, they just evaporate into nothing...

But is this what she meant? Is this what she meant when she told me to write her something?

How do we ever know what people really mean? What if she's wrong? Maybe I'm not a great writer. Maybe I'm stupid.

BLACKOUT

02

TERRY is now on the bed. He is still writing in his notebook and talking out loud.

TERRY:　　　Shall I write what happened yesterday? Or was it the day before? Or the day before that? I don't even know when that was.

Today. I should start with today.

Today I'm here. Today I'm writing. I love writing. Yes, that's the truth. When I write I feel free; I feel strong.

I don't feel useless. I don't feel crippled.

In words I can say everything, see everything, and do everything. Everything I can't say, do or see in the flesh. When I write I'm not afraid, I'm not afraid to understand.

Is this what I'm writing for her? My understanding? My understanding of everything?

Stick to the facts. Be practical.

I'm alone again. In the apartment. She's not here. She left. I tried the door. I think it's locked.

I think. Is it really locked? Or am I too weak to open it?

(TERRY goes to the door and tries to open it but he can't.)

I'm trying again right now. It moves, the latch, I think, it moves but it doesn't move all the way. I'm afraid to pull it more. It feels like I shouldn't pull it more. It feels like it does not intend me to pull it further.

Maybe because it is locked?

Did she lock me inside again?

Or am I afraid to leave the apartment again?

When she left, I screamed. I howled at her like a maniac. Told her to go fuck herself. Called her a slut and a cunt.

I did all of this silently of course. In total silence.

Those kinds of sounds don't come out of a mouth like mine too easily. But I do think I mustered a "fuck you." I remember struggling with the word "fuck."

I have no problem writing it. I just can't say it to somebody. But I did. I made an effort and as she was closing the door behind her I bet she could have heard me utter the words.

Fuck. You.

It felt good.

Then I masturbated.

Three times.

I came three times.

I came on her side of the bed.

On her pillow.

And on her clothes.

It felt good.

BLACKOUT

03

TERRY is more agitated than he was earlier. There are more papers and notebooks lying on the floor.

TERRY: She leaves. That's what she does. She always leaves. And then she comes back. Last time she came back, something happened.

Was it the last time she came back or some other time? I'm not sure. One of the times. One of the times she came back something happened.

I was here. I was alone. I was writing. And she arrived.

JENNIFER walks in and pauses at the door. TERRY inspects her.

TERRY: Was she wet? Was it raining? Was it the time she came in all wet from the rain?

JENNIFER takes off her jacket and starts making herself at home whilst looking around as if expecting something.

TERRY: Yes! She came in and expected food. Yes, now it's coming, that's what happened, this is what happened, it's like a scene, yes, I'm writing it down like a scene, like a script, this is her, this is Jennifer, and this is me, Terry *(he takes his position on the floor as in Scene 01).*

Jennifer walked in to find me here, on the floor, writing in my notebook.

JENNIFER: Hi honey. I'm so soaked!

TERRY: Hi.

JENNIFER pauses as if waiting for instructions, then she continues with her actions as TERRY narrates.

TERRY: She started taking her clothes off, the wet clothes, and I was writing, and I didn't feel like standing up, I didn't feel like giving her a hug and all that and kisses and all that. Why? Why didn't I do that? She was irritated and angry. As usual.

JENNIFER: I left the company. I'm done with those assholes.

TERRY: Mhm.

JENNIFER: That's all? You're not asking me why I left the company?

TERRY: Why did you leave the company?

JENNIFER: Because they're shit.

TERRY: I heard you say they were great.

JENNIFER: I was deceived. I thought they were a good company when I saw their take on Ibsen. But that was with another director, not this one. This one is shit, and the whole company is now shit.

TERRY: I thought you liked this director because it was a woman. You did say — *Finally, I'm going to be directed by a woman.*

JENNIFER: And again, deceived! Deceived by a stupid hack. It's easy to be hoodwinked by stupidity when you try to respect people. But I'm done respecting shits that don't deserve it.

TERRY: Mhm. (*Not giving her much attention.*)

JENNIFER: What are you doing?

TERRY: I'm writing.

JENNIFER: I need you to hear this, Terry.

TERRY: I'm all ears. What do you want me to hear?

JENNIFER: The woman wants to put up Strindberg! I couldn't believe it. Another fuckin Strindberg!

TERRY: What's wrong with Strindberg?

JENNIFER: He was a woman-hating son of a bitch, that's what's wrong with Strindberg! His most famous play ends with a woman being handed a knife by a guy to cut her own throat, and she does it!

TERRY: So, Strindberg is bad. Got it.

JENNIFER: I quit. And I quit for good from all of them. There's not a single company worth a shit. Nothing but hacks begging for bums on seats. I'm done.

TERRY: You must be right, they're all hacks.

He continues to write. JENNIFER is annoyed by his lack of engagement in the conversation.

JENNIFER: How was your day? How is your writing coming along?

TERRY: Aaahhmmm. Yeah. So and so. I don't think it's any good. Anyway, I need to write some more.

What was I writing? I was writing something I didn't want her to read, it must be in this other notebook. Where is it? What was I writing?

Oh yes! Here it is.

Crystal eating out Amanda's ass.

The pornographic images are projected onto the stage, no attempt needs to be made to make the images clear or well-framed, the image should be stretched out onto the entire acting space.

TERRY: Yes! That's it. Now I remember. Crystal was really going for Amanda's asshole. I was seeing this. Yes, before she came in, before Jennifer walked in, I was watching Crystal eating out Amanda and I was writing it down.

I didn't feel like talking to her about that. Anyway, first it was all about Strindberg, then

16

she wanted food. That's what she wanted, dinner, she asked me about dinner.

JENNIFER: What are we having for dinner?

TERRY: Pasta. There's some tomato sauce left over from yesterday.

JENNIFER: So where is it?

TERRY: What?

JENNIFER: The pasta? On the phone you said you're cooking for me.

TERRY: Oh, I meant later, I'm cooking later. I'll get to it, just need to finish this, then I'll cook.

Yes, that was it, she had called earlier, I told her I was cooking, or I cooked, or I was thinking of cooking? I did. I told her I was going to cook for her. That's what I said.

(He remembers. He writes it down.)

It was earlier. Jennifer called. She called to tell me she was coming home again.

JENNIFER picks up a phone and calls TERRY. He answers. The pornographic images are still playing.

JENNIFER: Hi honey.

TERRY: Jennifer. Are you okay? Where are you?

JENNIFER: Yes, yes, I'm fine. I'm with a friend, but I'm coming back home soon. Fuck, it's raining.

TERRY: I'll cook you something. Come and I'll cook you something.

JENNIFER: Yes, that would be lovely!

TERRY: I miss you.

JENNIFER   Me too, see you soon. Love you.

TERRY: Love you too. *(Back to the notebook.)* Or something like that. Anyway. By then a guy had walked in, yes, right as I was telling Jennifer I'll cook something for her, a guy had walked in, and he joined Amanda and Crystal in their activities. They turned their attention to him as soon as he showed up.

I wonder how that feels? That must feel good, no? Nice, right? How long had I been seeing them, these movies inside my head?

Must be in my other notebook, I've been documenting my fantasies for quite a while now. That's where I got the idea from. The idea to start documenting not only my fantasies, and my thoughts, but everything else.

Everything Jennifer says and does and everything I say to her and do, our behaviour, our scenes. For that's what this is all about, no? These are scenes, no? This is life, yes? One scene after another being played out, one second after another.

Writing, all of it is writing.

REWIND. JENNIFER leaves the apartment and the pornographic images rewind to the start.

04

FAST FORWARD. The pornographic images replay faster, following his narration, up to the point where JENNIFER comes back in.

TERRY: So that's how it happened. First, the phone call, no, first Amanda and Crystal eating ass, then the phone call, he comes in, I'm writing everything down and, and, time, time passes, I lose track of it, it just passes; minutes, hours, I don't know, then she arrives, yes, Jennifer comes in and I close one notebook and pick another one, I don't want her to see what I've been writing and I start writing something else and she talks.

JENNIFER: Hi honey. I'm so soaked!

TERRY: Hi.

              She's taking her wet clothes off. I didn't like that. And then she goes into her Strindberg rant.

JENNIFER: I left the company. Strindberg, Strindberg, Strindberg. Everybody stupid. I'm done.

TERRY: Something like that. And then she wanted to know what I was doing, and where was dinner, and that's where I got in trouble…

JENNIFER: How was your day? How is your writing coming along?

TERRY: Aaahhmmm. Yeah. So and so. I don't think it's any good. Anyway, I need to write some more.

JENNIFER: What are we having for dinner?

TERRY: Pasta. There's some tomato sauce left
                over from yesterday.

JENNIFER: So where is it?

TERRY: What?

JENNIFER: The pasta? On the phone you said
                you're cooking for me.

TERRY: Oh, I meant later, I'm cooking later. I'll
                get to it, just need to finish this, then I'll cook.

                She kept taking her clothes off and I could
                barely look at her. Let alone cook for her. I can
                see now she was really annoyed.

                Why can't I see these things immediately? In
                real time? Why do I only become aware of what
                others might have been feeling or thinking after
                the moment has passed? Always in hindsight.
                She was annoyed and pissed off and she put
                music on. *(she does)*

                So I put the music off. *(he does)*

                I said I'm trying to write.

JENNIFER: Okay, okay!

TERRY: I wanted her to leave. She had just arrived back and I wanted her to leave, but she kept talking. I wanted to go back to my writing. She wanted to talk.

JENNIFER: I started working on some ideas today, I'll show you later.

TERRY: I didn't reply. I hoped she would just shut up on her own. I prayed she would shut up and stop taking her clothes off and just, just…sit there or something. But things got worse. They always do. I always feel bad, I always want her to come back, then she does come back, and things get worse. They always do.

When was this? Was this yesterday? Three days ago? Five days ago? How long has she been gone again?

JENNIFER: Okay, I'll go take a shower, get this damn rain out of my hair…by then you'll hopefully be ready to have a proper conversation.

TERRY: I could barely look at her. She took the rest of her clothes off and went in the shower.

22

The sound of the shower comes on. She's showering. "Conversation" she said. She wanted to talk to me about something. What was it? What was happening? Was she leaving again? Panic attack.

What did you mean by that? What proper conversation? Is there something we need to talk about?

JENNIFER: I'm having a shower, would you mind?

TERRY: I want to know what you mean by that; did I do something wrong?

JENNIFER: I don't mean anything; I don't have anything to tell you.

TERRY: Can you please turn that water off, I'm trying to talk to you!

JENNIFER: Go back to your bloody writing and let me have a goddam shower!

TERRY: I don't feel like writing now, you broke my mood. I don't know what I'm writing anymore.

JENNIFER: Then take a break, cook something!

TERRY: I don't feel like cooking either. But I am hungry now. I feel like Chinese.

              I think she came out of the shower at some point, I don't remember hearing her turn the shower off. All I remember is that suddenly she was standing there; all wet and naked and totally pissed off. I didn't know where to look, I…

              The words, I can only stick to the words.

JENNIFER: Oh, you feel like some Chinese?

TERRY: Yes. Some lemon chicken, with fried rice? Can you cook me some?

JENNIFER: Jesus Christ Terry, you're unbelievable.

TERRY: No, no, no, you're right, I should cook, I said I'll cook something for you…but…

JENNIFER: But what?

TERRY: But…you know…I lose track of time. You know I lose track of time… I'm in this room all day, and I just…

JENNIFER: You're in here all day to write! You
              know that's why you stay in here, so you can
              focus on your writing, on what you do best.

TERRY: But I can't concentrate all the
              time…and…you haven't got any clothes on.
              Can you put some clothes on please?

JENNIFER: I don't have to put clothes on Terry,
              this is my home. And if you can't write all the
              time then do something different!

TERRY: She was getting closer, she was naked
              and wet and getting closer and I had nowhere
              to run…

              I'm sorry, I'm sorry, you're right…I need to
              focus more…stay active…stay sharp…I'm
              being an idiot again…

JENNIFER: No, you're not an idiot. You're a
              brilliant writer Terry, you know that. You just
              need the right conditions, the right inspiration.

TERRY: And she just picked up a towel. Oh
              thank God she did. She was drying herself in
              the towel, meaning she was about to put some

clothes on soon and I could put myself together again, somehow, a bit.

JENNIFER: We all need inspiration if we are to do something great. Even I need inspiration.

TERRY: What did she mean by that? Is this what she wanted to tell me? Is this the "conversation"? She did want to tell me something.

What do you mean by that? What are you trying to say? Don't I inspire you anymore?

JENNIFER: Of course you do. That's not how I meant it.

TERRY: You're not leaving me again are you? Please tell me you're not leaving me. Please tell me you still love me.

JENNIFER: Terry! I don't want you to talk like that. You know I love you.

JENNIFER lets the towel go again and she approaches TERRY fully nude. He's terrified.

TERRY: I need you Jennifer. You're all I have. But you don't have any clothes on...

JENNIFER: Come on Terry, you've seen me naked before. We talked about this. We talk about this, every day.

TERRY: You know how I feel…but I do love you…

JENNIFER: So, you shouldn't be afraid of me naked. I love you and you love me. And we're adults.

JENNIFER stops in a freeze and TERRY removes himself from her almost-embrace. Lights get dimmer until the stage is in darkness, JENNIFER can't be seen anymore. TERRY is left all alone in a dim spot.

TERRY: She was getting closer and I had nowhere to run. And then she…And then I…

And then she put her clothes on and ran out.

She left.

That was it. Yes. She just put her clothes on and ran out.

BLACKOUT

05

ONSCREEN

ARCHIVAL FOOTAGE – ONSITE INTERVIEW WITH SURVIVOR

A young woman is sobbing and shivering, sitting on the edge of an ambulance, pale-faced but sweaty.

JOURNALIST: You were at the scene of this horrible tragedy, can you tell us something about what just happened?

YOUNG WOMAN: I can't believe it. I just can't believe they shot her. It was a show, a play, that's all it was. We were just watching a play and they started shooting at us and for a second there I thought it was fake, part of the show, but the blood was real. Susan's blood, my friend Susan's blood was real. I tried pulling her, I told her to run with me but she didn't move, oh my God, she didn't move and was covered in blood, so I screamed and ran out. I left her in there and ran out and I heard other shots and other people screaming, everybody was running out. Is this real? Is this really happening?

FADE TO BLACK

06

TV NEWS FEATURE – THIS YEAR

JOURNALIST: On the twentieth of September, in 1995, Jennifer Cole and Terence F. Williams, staged the one and only performance of their experimental theatrical production *Quasar Love*. The show was not widely publicized, and it attracted a small local audience, but this was not the reason for its one and only staging. As the survivors of that night will never forget, towards the end of the performance Jennifer and Terence both appeared naked holding a loaded shotgun. Without any warning, they shot at the audience, killing four innocent viewers and grievously wounding two others before withdrawing themselves onstage where they took their own lives.

This year actors _________ and _________ shall be attempting to re-stage the performance of *Quasar Love* from an adaptation of the original notebooks. This decision has already raised some controversy, and many have spoken against the restaging of this performance out of respect for the victims. On today's episode of *Days of Infamy,* we have with us those who remember *Quasar Love* and are willing to share their bitter recollections.

FADE TO BLACK

07

ONSTAGE

TERRY is back on the floor, writing and talking.

TERRY: Where is she? Where does she go when she's not home? Is she coming back? When is she coming back? Do I want her to come back? What is taking her so long? Is it because of what I said? Did she believe me?

She must have known I was only joking; she must have known. How could she take me seriously? She knows I like to joke like that. Then again, she was naked. She knows I hate it when she takes her clothes off like that.

It's like she does it on purpose. I know she does it on purpose. Why, why does she keep doing that? When is she coming back? What is taking her so long?

Is it because of what I said? Or maybe because of what I've done? Did I do something? What have I done? Should I go look for her? Leave the apartment? Try the door?

It's useless. The door is useless. I can't open it. I can't leave. Wait. I just have to wait. She'll be back. Sooner or later, she'll be back.

I just have to write. Write everything. Write everything and she'll be back.

Where does "everything" start?

With explosions, explosions in space, stars die, and explode in space, and when stars die and explode, they leave holes, they leave giant holes behind them, and these giant holes sometimes become special, very special. The most special thing in the universe. The greatest thing in the universe.

Quasars.

(Images of space, stars, the cosmos are projected onto the stage.)

There's nothing more beautiful than quasars and I know a lot about them. I've written this already. It's here, somewhere here in this notebook.

Yes—in the sixties—or was it the fifties? — anyway, I wrote sixties here—I love this story, I want to read it, reading and writing, writing and reading—

In the 1960s, astronomers detected a set of radio waves in the night sky which led them to discover a source of luminescent intergalactic light. Back then, they had no explanation for their discovery. The light was simply too bright to be explained. It wasn't a star, and it certainly wasn't a planet. With their lack of information, they decided to call it a quasi-stellar object, and, in short, it was nicknamed the quasar. Today, even though quasars remain amongst the most mysterious of galactic bodies, we know much more about what these really are. The source of the strongest possible light in the known universe, quasars are enormous black holes known as supermassive black holes, hovering at the centre of distant galaxies. Yet something extremely peculiar happens in these black holes.

Usually, black holes simply absorb everything into their relentless gravitational pull and, as is common knowledge, nothing is ever able to escape a black hole's pull, including light itself, giving black holes their characteristic absolute blackness. Yet quasars have an amazing paradoxical feature; the supermassive black hole pulls in dust and matter at such speeds that the debris forms a spinning disc of breaking matter just before it all gets sucked into its vortex. This disc of spinning matter heats up enough to shoot out an unfathomable jet of radioactive light, a steady unstoppable stream of light capable of breaking through its own galaxy and travelling across the universe for millions of lightyears across space and time itself, straight into our very eyes.

It's amazing. Light shooting out of the darkness. Just like that. I wonder how it would feel to be there, right up there in outer space, and see it. See a quasar for real, up close. I think it would be wonderful. It would be crushing and fatal, but awfully wonderful.

BLACKOUT

08

TERRY: I lied. I said I masturbated, when she left, I mean. And I said I came three times. I wrote it. Here it is. I wrote—

Then I masturbated.

Three times.

I came three times.

I came on her side of the bed.

On her pillow.

And on her clothes.

It felt good.

But I didn't. I wish I did. But no. I didn't. I don't do that. My body doesn't do that. You need to feel things to do that and I don't. I do, I do feel things, but not like that. I know how it works. I know how bodies work and what bodies do.

I have fantasies. I do. I imagine naked people doing all sorts of things to themselves and each other. You see, I know what naked people look like. I know what they do to each other.

When I was young, my brother, Robert, used to show me things. He used to show me skin flicks. That's what he called them. Skin flicks. Because you saw a lot of skin. All of it. Of every part of the body.

We had a VHS player and Mom and Dad used to go out a lot and leave me with him.

He was sixteen, I was eight. He used to show me the skin flicks, tell me I had to see those films to become a man. *That's what you'll be doing when you grow up*, he told me. *That's it. Look at them.*

At first, I didn't want to look. *I don't like it* I said. But he insisted. *You're a bit simple,* he said. *You need to see it to learn, you'll never learn on your own. Come on, don't be an idiot. Watch.*

And so, I watched.

I looked at all the dicks and cunts and tits and asses and mouths and spit and cum that he showed me. Years. He showed me all this for years on end. Year after year after year, watching skin flicks during our spare time.

Sometimes he would leave me alone to watch and he'd go out. I always hated going out, so he'd put on a video for me and leave. And I'd sit there, and watch.

Now I don't need videos anymore. I just see things. All I need to do is think of things and see them. They just come to my mind. So, I see them and I write them down in this notebook. Just like this.

(The corresponding images are projected onto the stage.)

Joseph and David, two best friends, are doing their homework together. They are at David's house because David's mom and dad both work late, so David and Joseph always have three or four hours of privacy after school and they love studying together. Or at least that's how it always starts. First, they meet to study and do their homework together but that doesn't last long. They never work for too long. Not on their homework. Joseph has the fatter of the two dicks and David loves having it in his mouth. David was always the one to give head for longer. Joseph, on the other hand, loves…

NO. NO. NO. NO. NO.

I shouldn't be seeing this one.

I shouldn't be writing this one.

NOT THIS ONE.

My brother said these ones are not for men. No. Not for men like us.

He showed me one, only once, he did. He showed me one with two men in it, they were putting their cocks in each other's mouth and in each other's ass but he said it was just as a warning. Just to make sure I knew what I shouldn't do. What I should never think of.

Then he showed me one where three guys had a very young girl for a very long time. And they did things to her. Lots of things. Lots of things everywhere. Until she spat and gagged and almost choked to death. He said, *That's it. That's how men do it. That's what real men do.*

BLACKOUT

09

ONSCREEN

ARCHIVAL FOOTAGE - INTERVIEW WITH ROBERT WILLIAMS, BROTHER OF TERENCE F. WILLIAMS

BROTHER: No, I can't believe it. My brother could have never been able to do something like that. He was a shy, caring young man. I refuse to believe it.

JOURNALIST: We are trying to better understand what might have happened; what might have led your brother to get involved in this tragedy. Is there anything in his past that was telling of violent behaviour?

BROTHER: My brother? Violent? He was always a bit simple and a bit of a weirdo I'll give you that, but not violent. He loved science books, and watching movies but he was never good at school, he was…as I said, a simple person, know what I mean? Maybe he was stubborn at times, yes, that's why he left home. He didn't have to leave, I never kicked him out. Even when Mom and Dad died, I took care of him. He was shy and a bit crazy at times but…not violent. Never. My brother wouldn't have hurt a fly. It must have been her. It must have been her fault. I'm sure she put him up to it. My brother could have never done such a horrible thing on his own. I'll refuse to believe it. It's her fault. It must be.

FADE TO BLACK

10

ONSTAGE

TERRY is very agitated.

TERRY: Where is she? Why hasn't she come back yet? Is she happy? Does she miss me?

Maybe she's happier when she's not with me. Maybe that's why she stays away for so long. But that's okay. I get it. She can't be with me all the time.

She has ambitions. Jennifer has ambitions.

She's creative; an artist, an actress, a director, she's amazing. I know she is. She just needs to find that one thing, that one idea, that great piece of work to break into the scene. That's why she is sad. She is always sad, angry and frustrated, because she hasn't found it yet, not yet. Not that great thing, not yet.

JENNIFER enters the room and sits on the bed.

She says we can do it. She says together we can find it, create it even.

JENNIFER & TERRY (in unison): Together we can show them all what we're capable of. We have to appease them, impress them, blow their minds even. Because we need their recognition, their appreciation, that's the unfortunate truth; we need them, yet we hate them.

TERRY: That's what Jennifer told me. Then she said:

JENNIFER: Everybody is on TV. They love you if you're on TV. No matter how fuckin' thick you are. I had a friend once, at drama school,

Mildred. Snotty fuckin' Mildred—she thought Beckett needed more plot.

TERRY: And?

JENNIFER: She's on TV! Another shit soap.

TERRY: So what?

JENNIFER: So, everybody is seeing her and talking about her and saying how great she is! And here we are, nobodies; three, five, ten times the intelligence and talent and ideas of snotty Mildred and nobody knows we even exist.

TERRY: But how do you know we are better than your friend? How can you say that we are more deserving?

JENNIFER: Don't be so naïve Terry! Of course we are! I've read your work and I've shown you some of my ideas; it's good stuff. Our work is great. But it never achieves any real success, now does it? Just because we don't suck up to them and write everything all smiles and giggles for their fat, dumb asses.

TERRY: You have new projects, you are working on new things, no? You keep trying.

JENNIFER: Every little thing I do is rejected or put on hold. Nothing is working! I've never made a single cent from my work!

TERRY: But you do make money, no? You bring stuff home and you pay the rent, so how do you…

JENNIFER: That's different Terry. You know I don't like talking about that. You know you shouldn't ask me questions about that. How I pay the rent is none of your business!

TERRY: I'm sorry, I shouldn't have brought it up.

JENNIFER: But I need something Terry, I need something new and different! Please, write me something. I know you're good, I know you've got it in you. Write something crazy! Something that will make us famous, something that will make us great.

TERRY: Famous? Really? You want to be another face on TV? Is that who you think you are?

JENNIFER: It's not just about TV. It's about…It's about this need. You know, this deep need to be recognized, that desire you feel for others to look at you and deem you worthy, deem you of value. I need that Terry, I need the whole world to know me and make me feel great, and give me meaning.

TERRY: But you already mean something. You mean a lot, to me. You are my whole world.

JENNIFER: Aaaw Terry, you're so sweet. We do have each other. But it still doesn't feel like it's enough. I still feel empty and useless. We could be having so much more. Much more. Once they see us, and recognize how amazing we are, then we'll have it all, everything we deserve, we'll have all of it. And we'll stop feeling like shit all the fuckin' time.

TERRY: But how do we do that?

JENNIFER: By impressing them. I need something to direct, something to put onstage, something to show them. Something to grab their attention with and never let go! Write me something

Terry. Please, write me something that will change my life forever.

JENNIFER freezes on the spot.

11

Then she turns around, giving the audience her back. As TERRY says the following lines, she starts taking her clothes off until she's in the nude, in time to coincide with TERRY's narrative where she continues to act out what he is saying.

TERRY: That feels like such a long time ago. *Write me something Terry,* she said. And I'm writing. I'm still writing. But where is she? Why isn't she back yet? How long has it been? Three days? Five days? Ten?

Should I go look for her? The door. I can't open the door.

She was here. Right here. Without any clothes on. And then she left. Why did she leave? What happened? What did I say? What did I do?

She was right here, walking towards me naked. She said we were both adults. She said she loved me. I was terrified. She said—

JENNIFER: Terry, please let me touch you. Stop being afraid. There's nothing to be afraid of.

TERRY: I'm not afraid!

JENNIFER: Then let me kiss you. I love you. I'm here for you. I want you to be happy.

TERRY: If you want me to be happy, then stay away from me!

JENNIFER: You want me to leave? You want me gone?

TERRY: No! I love you and I want you here but I don't want you so…so close…

JENNIFER: Then you *are* afraid of me!

TERRY: I said I'm not afraid of you! I'm not afraid of…of a naked girl!

JENNIFER: I'm not a girl! I'm a woman, and you're a man, and I love you and you love me and we're living together, and I want you inside of me.

JENNIFER freezes again and the lights go off, leaving only a spot on TERRY extremely agitated now.

TERRY: And that's when I hit her.

From the darkness, we can hear JENNIFER cry every time she's hit.

That's what I did. I hit her. Because she was naked and being a slut, so I hit her in the face. I hit her in the face, and I threw her down and I hit her again and again and I held her and…and I did things to her…bad things…

TERRY's vigour is wearing off and he's looking for words.

And I…

And she…

And then she…

And then she…left…

She put her clothes on and left. And she hasn't been back since.

BLACKOUT

End of Act One

Act Two

12

ONSCREEN

INTERVIEW WITH THEATRE OWNER – THIS YEAR

JOURNALIST: Mr Gladwell, what do you remember about the events on the night of *Quasar Love*?

THEATRE OWNER: I was in the control booth doing the lights and the sound for the show. Back then I did tech in the theatre, I did everything really. I owned the place, managed it, the works. I rented the place out for all kinds of shows and I knew that these younger kids were trying out all sorts of crazy things, but who could have predicted that?

JOURNALIST: So there were never any signs that things could go horribly wrong on this production?

THEATRE OWNER: All productions show signs that things can go wrong. You always have the sulky introverted one with anger management issues, the megalomaniacal diva, the control

freak, the micromanaging asshole, this is
theatre! We meet and work with all sorts of
sensitive people all the time. Doesn't mean we
expect them to take out a loaded gun and start
shooting at people.

JOURNALIST:　　　　　What about during rehearsals?

THEATRE OWNER:　　There were no rehearsals. We
never ran through the whole thing. We just did
some quick light and sound checks and that
was it. The piece was supposed to be based on
a lot of improvisation and readings from the
texts that Terence Williams was working on.
From the little I understood, Jennifer wanted the
show to be an experimental reading of sorts; this
wasn't your regular kind of performance at all.
Terence was onstage, very anxious to be there
mind you, and he was reading from these
apparently autobiographical notes of his, and
Jennifer was coming in and out of the scenes
that referred to her. But then they took the gun
out and things started going haywire.

JOURNALIST:　　　　　What did you do when you
saw the gun?

THEATRE OWNER: At first, I was simply pissed off. As I was the theatre owner hosting the show, I should have been told about that kind of thing, and I was already not so happy that they had started taking their clothes off. I wasn't told about all the nudity either, but I just thought I would give them a talking to after the performance. Nudity sells tickets anyway.

JOURNALIST: And then?

THEATRE OWNER: And then he loaded the damn thing and started shooting at the audience.

JOURNALIST: Did you think it was a special effect?

THEATRE OWNER: I know special effects when I see them. That sound and that blood, it was no special effect. And, anyway, they wouldn't have had the chance to install something like that without me knowing it or helping them. I immediately put the fire alarm on, called the police and ran the hell out of there. The audience took a few seconds more to react, some of them did think it was part of the show, initially. But then someone started screaming, the fire alarm was on, everybody went into a total panic and mayhem ensued. I did not see all of it since I could do nothing but run.

JOURNALIST: Were you scared?

THEATRE OWNER: Scared? I shat myself! I ran and ran until I locked myself at home. I still have nightmares about it sometimes.

JOURNALIST: You abandoned your theatre?

THEATRE OWNER: Without giving it a second thought! I was terrified I tell you. And I knew I had all the fire and emergency exits in good service so I just hoped that everybody would make it out alive. Unfortunately, not all of them did.

JOURNALIST: This year, *Quasar Love* is being restaged by two performers who have found the original notebooks used by Jennifer Cole and Terence Williams. Do you have any thoughts on that?

THEATRE OWNER: Why? Can't we just try and forget this horrible thing ever happened? I think

it's perverse, truly perverse to want to restage
that show. It should be stopped.

CUT TO

13

INTERVIEW WITH GRIEVOUSLY WOUNDED
SURVIVOR – THIS YEAR

JOURNALIST: You were injured on the night
        of the *Quasar Love* tragedy, correct?

SURVIVOR: Yes. I lost most functionality of my right
        arm, almost lost the arm completely, actually,
        because they considered amputating it full-stop,
        but then the doctors saved what they could.

JOURNALIST: Did Terence Williams shoot at
        you directly?

SURVIVOR: No. I don't know whether he was
        shooting at specific people or just at the audience
        in general. I was hit by the same blast that killed the
        guy sitting right next to me. Since the shotgun blast
        opens up into a wider radius the further it travels,
        by the time it hit the front row from the stage it was
        wide enough to hit a couple of seated people, and
        unfortunately still kill someone.

JOURNALIST: Do you remember the moment you were shot at?

SURVIVOR: It was insane. I still can't believe that moment ever happened. We could tell something was wrong and that this was not a normal performance, but nobody would expect such a thing. The performance had been going on for an hour or so and by that time, both actors had stripped each other naked onstage. They had been reading from these notebooks and performing what looked like intimate scenes, and there had already been a couple of moments where they had this shotgun in their hands, but nobody would even consider the possibility that it wasn't a prop. Then, as it was coming to an end, Terence and Jennifer came together, completely naked, holding the gun between them, Terence simply pointed the thing at us and shot.

JOURNALIST: It must have been horrible.

SURVIVOR: It was of course but, funnily enough, that's not how I would describe it. What followed after was a total nightmare, but that first shot, even though I myself got badly maimed by it, gave this sense of… How shall I describe it? It was a heightened experience of sorts, I don't know, I don't want to sound like some new age mystic or something, but I saw these two naked people in front of me right there onstage, right? And I was in the front row, and suddenly a loud bang, a flash of light, the abrupt searing pain in my right arm, and I became immediately aware of this long second of silence, but a very different kind of silence. It wasn't a silence due to lack of sound. For that incredible second, I could feel my heart thumping, I could feel the blood flowing out of my wounds, Jennifer and Terence holding the gun and looking down at us… I felt myself in the presence of something otherworldly, something I had never experienced before. And then somebody started screaming, Terence started shooting again and all hell broke loose.

JOURNALIST: What do you think about the idea of restaging *Quasar Love*? Do you think it should be performed again?

SURVIVOR: Is it? Is it going to happen again?

JOURNALIST: Yes, it's being restaged this year. Do you think it should be done?

SURVIVOR: I think it's dangerous. I don't know. I'm definitely not going to see it, but I think that to take two actors and put them in the shoes of Jennifer and Terence, it's not safe.

JOURNALIST: But isn't that what actors do? Step in the shoes of others, including dangerous or deranged people?

SURVIVOR: I don't know. *Quasar Love* was real, and people died because of that show. Shouldn't there be limits? Why take the risk?

FADE TO BLACK

14

TERRY and JENNIFER are standing still, side by side, centre-stage.

JENNIFER: I became fascinated by quasars as soon as Terry told me their story. How could such a duality take shape in the same celestial object?

TERRY: The ultimate destructive force in the known universe, the supermassive black hole, a phenomenon that knows no parallel in both scale and devastation, produces the ultimate light, the ultimate source of energy, believed to be involved in the very birth of entire galaxies.

JENNIFER: Destruction and creation.

TERRY: Dark and light.

JENNIFER: Gargantuan physical bodies in the heavens playing forth the very narrative our irrelevant minuscule human existence has been trying to grasp and comprehend since our genesis here on Earth. Our kind is merely putting in new words, decorating and spelling out in new forms and shapes, a narrative which is not only beyond humanity but applies to the entirety of material existence.

TERRY: I can't help but ask, where is my place in this narrative? What is my role? Am I the light propelled into the darkness? Am I the debris, the dead and the broken, falling into the eternal hole?

JENNIFER: Or am I the black hole itself? Could I be the very darkness, forever hungry, forever swallowing and engulfing, breaking and churning the life out of everything and everyone I come in contact with?

TERRY: She's gone again. I'm alone again. Things were better. For a while.

She gave me a present and it's beautiful and terrifying. I just don't know what to do with it. I have no idea. I don't know how to hold it, I don't know how to use it, or when or where or why.

It's insane. Why did she bring that thing in here? Anyway, we put the box under the bed and left it there. I think not even she knows why she brought it.

Where has she been? What kind of people has she been messing about with?

In truth, I didn't care. She was back and she wasn't trying to kiss me or taking her clothes off in front of me or any of that sex shit. It was good.

And we talked. We talked a lot. We talked for days. And I wrote most of it down, but I can't always keep up and sometimes I forget things, or I change things, or I don't even know if I am changing things or not. I tried my best.

And I was reading a lot. Reading everything I was writing. Reading Jennifer. Reading myself. Reading myself reading Jennifer.

It's not just writing. Not all of it. It's also reading. Writing and reading. What we create, what we say, what we put in motion is all the writing. What we absorb, what we hear, what we see, what we observe and listen to, that's all reading. Writing and reading. Reading and writing.

All of existence as we may know it, all of life as we may know it. Reading and writing, writing and reading, on and on and on… And for a short while, it was fine.

Where is she now? Where is Jennifer? Why is she gone again? Is she doing this to me on purpose?

Am I going insane? Is she driving me insane?

BLACKOUT

15

A medium-sized box, larger than a shoe box but smaller than a chest, is now in the middle of the stage. TERRY and JENNIFER are in a tender embrace in front of the box.

TERRY: I'm sorry, please don't leave me again.

JENNIFER: I'm sorry too. I shouldn't have put so much pressure on you.

TERRY: But I hurt you. I know I did. And I didn't mean to, I just didn't know what to do, what you were asking of me, and I lose control, I just stop thinking…

JENNIFER: Stop worrying about it. I got you a present. Something new. Something exciting.

TERRY: A present?

JENNIFER: Yes. I got it from a friend of mine who knew somebody and they wanted to get rid of it. They thought it might make a cool prop for a play or something but it's real. It's totally real. And we might get in trouble for having it, but, so fucking what? I think it's cool.

TERRY: What is it? Is it in the box?

JENNIFER: Yes. It's in the box. You can open it.

TERRY approaches the box, lifts the lid and looks at what's inside.

TERRY: That is…exciting.

BLACKOUT

16

JENNIFER is once again on the bed. TERRY is on the floor.

TERRY: *We'll go onstage together*, she said.

JENNIFER: You have to write something for both of us to act.

TERRY: But I can't act. You know I can't act. I can barely leave the apartment.

JENNIFER: This will be different. You'll see. This will be something you've written. We'll take what you're writing and, somehow, we'll put it onstage. It will be you and I, together. It will be great.

TERRY: I don't know about this. I'm afraid and shy and you know me… You can't trust me, Jennifer.

JENNIFER: I trust you'll be your amazing self. We'll give them something they've never seen.

TERRY: Will I have lines? Will I have to learn lines by heart?

JENNIFER: You can read. You can read from your notebooks.

TERRY: I didn't think of that. Still, what can we
                    do? I mean, I'm writing, but…

                    She was getting too close again… Why does she
                    always have to get so excited?

JENNIFER: Have you written something for me
                    Terry? *(trying to get closer to him)*

TERRY: Yes, I'm writing, but it's not ready yet
                    and I don't know what it is really…

JENNIFER: I liked your quasars stuff. Blackholes and
                    light and death and destruction. It's about the big
                    things in life, the enormity of it all. You're like one
                    of the greats Terry.

TERRY: The greats?

JENNIFER: Yes, the greats, the visionaries—Van
                    Gogh, Shakespeare—giving the world great
                    images and asking the big questions!

TERRY: Like—to be or not to be?

JENNIFER: Yes, just like that. Why are we in this
                    world? *What* are we in this world? Are we
                    believers? Are we destroyers? Why shouldn't we
                    just end it all?

60

TERRY: Yes…the big questions…I guess. *(clearly unconvinced)*

JENNIFER: I want to read more.

TERRY: Not now. Not today. You can't read more today.

JENNIFER: When then? When the fuck can I read something? *(very snappy)*

JENNIFER freezes on the spot.

TERRY: I felt like hitting her again. Knocking her unconscious. The things I'd love to do to her.

Tie her up. Hands behind her back, head tied down, gagged, blindfolded, on her knees. I'd spend days observing her holes. See how deep they go. Look for treasures deep inside of her.

Observe her twitch and squeeze and squirt as she loses control over all bodily functions, because she will, after enough time, after enough time just hanging there, tied and gagged and blindfolded, for days on end, her body will start deteriorating and everything will start going to waste.

Then I'd start experimenting. See with what I can fill her up. See what I can put in her.

I wonder when she'd die.

Or what of. Or maybe not. Maybe she'd love it. Maybe she'd enjoy every second of it and the very pain and degradation would keep her alive against all biological odds.

I'm feeling something and I recognize the need and it kind of feels good. I think I need to masturbate.

This is the first time I've wanted to masturbate in, what, eight, ten years? It's the idea, the idea of her dying that's making me feel this.

TERRY takes the still motionless JENNIFER and positions her on the bed like a mannequin. He puts her on her knees, bent forward, head down, hands stretched as if tied behind her back. Then he positions himself on top of her, standing on the bed, feet astride, with her beneath him, and starts masturbating.

TERRY: Or Jennifer almost dying. Jennifer gagged, blindfolded, seconds away from oblivion, all holes filled and emptied and filled over and over and over again.

Hours, days, months. Years of Jennifer enjoying me inside of her.

But it's not working. I can't feel it. My body just doesn't react.

I need to try. I need to try harder.

TERRY gives up on masturbating and JENNIFER gets up, pulls the box from underneath the bed, leaves it in the middle of the room and leaves.

Nothing. Still nothing. I need something else. My body is not enough.

I am feeling things, I feel things brewing inside of me, but my body is not enough, on its own, my body is not enough to react to everything I'm feeling.

TERRY stumbles onto the box in surprise. He opens it, and looks inside.

TERRY: I need something more.

DIM lights onstage. Throughout the next two interviews, TERRY is still moving on stage in a DIM light. He takes out the shotgun from the box. He looks at the weapon and holds it with respect. He loads the gun before he sits down in a cross-legged pose, centre-stage. He then holds the shotgun upright below his chin, with the

*barrel of the gun pressed against his jaw and puts a finger on the
trigger. He remains silent in this position all throughout onscreen
scenes 17 and 18.*

17

ONSCREEN

INTERVIEW WITH PSYCHOLOGIST – THIS
YEAR

JOURNALIST: Doctor, the theatre community
here has suffered a terrible tragedy, a heart-
wrenching blow if one might add, and you
yourself were among the survivors. How can we
make sense of this horror?

PSYCHOLOGIST: I was fortunate enough to be
sitting at the back of the small theatre, so even
though the moment was, of course, traumatic, I
did not experience the horror like those in the front
rows. I ran out as soon as I realized that the gunfire
was real, and I stayed at the door outside helping
people. From that point of view, being at the door
and hearing the rest of the following gunshots as
audience members ran out clambering and
crying in terror, I truly experienced something I

had never seen before. This was a real theatre of cruelty.

JOURNALIST: What did you see?

PSYCHOLOGIST: I saw their faces, the faces of the ones making it out alive, paraded in front of me as they came through the door one after the other, some throwing up, some covered in their own tears and snot, some totally ashamed for having defecated and urinated on themselves as they heard the gunshots being fired at their back, and yet, as you have rightly asked me, we have to make sense of it. We have to give it some form of meaning to live through it and move on. But how, what meaning?

JOURNALIST: Indeed, but since then, have you come to any new conclusions?

PSYCHOLOGIST: As I was seeing the performance, I was already struggling with understanding what these two characters, people, performers maybe, were attempting to do onstage. It was difficult to understand whether they were sharing with us their pain or accusing us of it. It was as if they were suggesting that, by our very nature, by being an audience, by expecting, demanding to be entertained whilst we remain observant and judgemental, we are already guilty. We are guilty of being an audience. I wish that Jennifer and Terence could have found a way of making us aware of this without claiming lives, both of others and their own, but I believe that we should consider what they were trying to tell us. So many out there hate this life, hate this world, mainly because they suffer, most of them unjustly, terribly so, simply because the rest of us choose to be an audience, choose to watch and judge without giving much back in return. We just go on doing what we always do hoping that the pain of these others will never reach us. But what if it does?

CUT TO

18

INTERVIEW WITH THEATRE CRITIC – THIS YEAR

JOURNALIST: Professor Eliot, it has always been the theatre's very nature to push the boundaries of what can and cannot be done onstage for the audience and in a very direct way, "to" the audience. Do you think that this very reason alone makes theatre a more "dangerous" art form?

CRITIC: I wish we didn't have to use the word "dangerous," though theatre is in a precarious position indeed, especially after recent events. Of all art forms, only theatre pits the audience with the artists together in such an intimate relationship with that degree of freedom. You are literally locking yourself up with these people in a room and, even though you might have some idea on what is about to happen or what should happen, the truth is that whatever is going to happen depends on these living, breathing people right there in that room with you. Whether they deliver something totally boring or make you laugh or make you excited or sad relies entirely on the actions and gestures and words that are truly happening right there and then.

JOURNALIST: Yet this is the very thing that makes theatre such an exciting art form, no?

CRITIC: Yes, indeed, but this also means that theatre is always trapped in a double bind; theatre needs to make the audience feel safe, safe that it is going to be entertained and shown a good time and given a good experience; yet theatre also needs to push itself into new directions, directions that, on occasion, need to explore the darker and more painful realities of our times. And this might not always be the "safe" thing to do.

JOURNALIST: Still, we can surely control how "unsafe" it can get…

CRITIC: The immediacy of theatre will always magnify its effects in unpredictable degrees. A boring piece of theatre can be a hundred times more boring than a movie, and a painful piece of theatre may truly be an experience of suffering and torment for both the actors onstage and the audience. For these reasons, theatre audiences will keep dwindling as time goes by, because only the truly brave and open—open of heart and of mind—will keep finding the courage to go to the theatre. Unfortunately, all of this becomes an even more ridiculously horrendous scenario if our audience is also risking actual death.

JOURNALIST: So would you say that what happened in the *Quasar Love* tragedy was a result of an extreme form of theatre? Was that all still a work of art?

CRITIC: Up until people started dying, yes, it was art. But once people started dying, a line was stepped over, a pact was broken. At that point, it was no longer theatre, it became a betrayal.

FADE TO BLACK

19

ONSTAGE

By the end of scene 19 TERRY leaves his position, unloads the gun, puts it back in the box and under the bed. JENNIFER returns and sits on the floor. TERRY looks at her.

TERRY: Maybe I am the black hole. I am the black hole sucking her in, every time she comes near me, I suck her in and she's always trying to escape, trying to breach my gravitational pull.

Maybe I'm destroying her, grinding her to pieces as I draw her near, breaking her down, molecule by molecule, atom by atom, the closer she gets the further she disintegrates until there's nothing left but space dust.

Space dust.

Contemplate the beauty of space dust. We were once nothing but space dust. And when our universe collapses back on itself again we will return to that very state.

Space dust.

Is that why I can't fuck her? Because deep down, I know, that she is nothing but space dust? Who fucks space dust? Who fucks Jennifer Cole?

BLACKOUT

20

JENNIFER: When can I read something?

TERRY: What? Read what?

JENNIFER: Some of your new stuff. You're writing a lot Terry. It's amazing. I don't think I've ever seen you writing this much. I'm sure you must be onto something great. May I have one of your new notebooks to read from?

TERRY: No. Not yet. I don't know yet.

JENNIFER: Why not? Aren't we supposed to be working together?

TERRY: But this is different. This writing is
                different, it is something new, it is something
                much more intimate and real and I don't want
                anybody seeing it yet. I don't think I'll ever let
                anybody see this. Not even you.

                I saw her face change. It was as if the life were
                being sucked right out of her. She looked at me
                and just opened her mouth. I don't even know
                whether she knew what she was saying or not or
                whether I was understanding what she was
                saying or not, but the words came out all leaden
                and heavy and dead.

JENNIFER: I don't get anything from you, Terry.
                Nothing. You give me nothing.

TERRY: Then she put on a short dress, put some
                makeup on and left.

BLACKOUT

21

The box is onstage once more.

TERRY: Now that I'm alone again, I'm doing it a
                lot. I open the box, take it out and look at it. It's

beautiful. I guess it must be a power thing, you know?

All this force, delivered with such brute potency, and all I need to do is squeeze a little trigger. Its effects are of course a matter of contemplation. The ease with which such a readily available thing could deprive a human being of life is awe-inspiring.

Terrifying, sure, but wonderfully so.

Yesterday I took it out, loaded it, held the barrel underneath my chin, put my finger on the trigger and waited, just waited. I'm still not sure whether I was waiting for something to happen or waiting for myself to do something. Maybe I don't even know the difference. But nothing happened. I waited for hours with the barrel under my chin and my finger on the trigger, and nothing happened.

I was doing it again this morning. I was doing it again right now. All morning, right now. Hours. I did it for hours.

I was sitting on the bed, holding the barrel to my chin, my finger on the trigger and I had lost all track of time. I had no idea, none at all, of how long I must have been there. With it like that. At one point, I was starting to become afraid that I was going to fall asleep, nod off and maybe then my finger would squeeze slightly on the metal and hellfire would rise up to shred my face into a pulp, make me faceless. A faceless mess of blood and bone. But as these thoughts ran through my head, I heard something. I focused on it. I didn't open my eyes since I did not want to break my concentration. But I focused hard and I was sure that I could hear breathing.

JENNIFER comes in and stops at the door, looking at TERRY.

TERRY: It was Jennifer. I'm sure. She was there, at the door, seeing me, quietly, silently. She did not interrupt me, she did not talk to me, but I could hear her breathing, I could smell the cigarette smoke that weaves itself in the room every time she comes home. She was there. And for some reason, I felt at ease. I felt a sense of comfort, knowing that she was present, knowing that she was overseeing my despair.

For a very brief moment, I felt loved.

JENNIFER exits.

TERRY: Then I heard the door close again and knew she was gone. I opened my eyes and there was no one there. She isn't back yet. But I am sure she was here.

She was.

I am.

She will be again.

BLACKOUT

22

TERRY is asleep in the bed. JENNIFER enters quietly, on tiptoes and she takes all his notebooks and leaves again. TERRY wakes up with a fright, but he's all alone.

TERRY: She took me by surprise. I was asleep, and she walked in, stealthily, I don't know, I didn't see her but she walked in, she came quietly as I lay asleep and took them all!

Every single notebook.

I woke up in an immediate frenzy.

The notebooks. *My* notebooks. All gone. I only have one left, the one I hold in my hands as I sleep. She didn't take this one.

First thing I thought was to run out, maybe she was still there, still behind the door, still walking away.

But the door. I can't deal with the door. I ran to it, struggled with it, banged on it, but it wouldn't open.

Did I forget? Did I forget how to open a door? Or is it locked?

Maybe it is. Maybe she came, took all my notebooks, locked the door, turned the key ten times and threw it in the river. Maybe I'll be locked in here forever. Maybe she'll never be back. If she comes back, I'll kill her. I will. I'll hit her, and fuck her to death. I'll fuck her with it. I'll fuck her with it and pull the trigger inside of her. See her explode.

I bet she'd like that.

BLACKOUT

The box is onstage. TERRY is on the floor. JENNIFER comes in and performs in silence everything that TERRY is saying.

TERRY: I still do not know whether I've seen this or dreamt it. Or maybe I felt it, I felt it happen right beside me as I slept and that's how I dreamt of it. She was here. Last night she was here.

I did not move, I stayed in bed, just stayed in bed quietly as she came in and took out the big white box from under the bed. She took out the box, opened it and looked inside.

Then she took it out.

She held it in her hands and touched it, felt its weight, it was as if she was fascinated by it. I could share her excitement; even though my eyes were closed and I was not wholly in this world, I could feel it all, as if I could feel through her own hands, share her excitement behind her own eyelids, inside her own skin.

She was so beautiful, in the dark, with a sliver of moonlight across her face, holding the metal in both her hands.

Then she did it! I almost leapt out of the bed to ask her how it felt, but I didn't want to ruin the moment. I know how delicately beautiful the moment is, anything, even a whisper may ruin it.

She sat on the edge of the bed, just by my feet, and she held it to her chin just like I do and she waited. She must have felt so alive. I wish so much I could talk to her about it. But it would spoil it. Talking about it like that would spoil it. Such a moment deserves much more, deserves much better.

She knows, I'm sure she knows. We cannot spoil it. Not this. This brings us together. This connects us in ways we could never imagine possible. Metal and fire. Metal and fire and flesh and blood. She's coming back. I know she is. Maybe I won't kill her. I don't know. Maybe I will, maybe I won't.

What if she wants it? What if she asks for it?

BLACKOUT

24

JENNIFER reads the notebooks on the bed as TERRY answers her questions.

TERRY: She's beautiful. As soon as I saw her again, that's all I could think. She's beautiful and she's reading my notebooks. When I woke up, I found her right in front of me, sitting there, reading my notebooks. Like in a dream.

JENNIFER: Is this us?

TERRY doesn't answer.

This is us... Is this our fight, is this what happened last time?

TERRY: Yes, our fight, warts and all. What you said, what I said, what you did, what I did, everything.

JENNIFER: What are you writing here, Terry?

TERRY: This is what I'm writing, this is the project I'm calling *Quasar Love.*

JENNIFER: Isn't *Quasar Love* the one about the black holes? What have we got to do with it?

TERRY: Yes, quasars are part of it, but it isn't just about quasars. I wanted to write about something more human, about what we do to each other and how we live together. It's documentation. I'm documenting "us," our reading and our writing, our love.

JENNIFER: Are you taking notes right now?

TERRY: Yes, this conversation will be in it too. I'm taking down notes on what we are saying so I may actually script it in full later.

JENNIFER: This is our life, we are living right now, we are not writing, this is us talking.

TERRY: I believe that this very moment is writing. All of human life is writing; reading and writing. Think about it; to live *is* to read and write.

JENNIFER: I'm not sure I'm following…

TERRY: Talking, acting, being…is writing; everything we express and act out and do is writing, we are writing out our scenes as we live them on this intergalactic manuscript called existence. And everything we take in, everything we observe, everything we listen to, is reading.

This is all that life is, reading and writing, writing and reading.

JENNIFER: You can't boil down the entirety of human experience to reading and writing, there's more to it than that.

TERRY: Why not? I think I can.

JENNIFER: If you are writing about us then you are writing about me, and I know that I feel much more complex!

TERRY: You feel complex but you're not, you're actually very simple.

JENNIFER: Do you have any idea how goddamn insulting that is?

TERRY: I did not mean it like that! I mean we feel complex because we are seeing it and feeling it all from the inside. Once it is all eviscerated and put on paper, or, say, onstage, like you want to, you will realize how much simpler it actually is.

JENNIFER: We are not onstage Terry; we are not in front of an audience right now.

TERRY: But what if we were?

JENNIFER: I don't know, I don't know what to do with this Terry! And there are intimate things, very intimate things in this, and you are lying. You are changing things and lying. You wrote that you hit me? Hit me? When did you ever hit me? When did I ever leave you because you hit me?

TERRY: I, I don't know, it felt easier to write, it felt like the scene made more sense like that than to write down what actually happened.

JENNIFER: You did not hit me Terry. I stood there, naked in front of you and asked you to fuck me and you said no. *So hit me* I said, that's what *I* asked for, I wanted you to hit me. *If you can't fuck me,* I said, *then hit me.* And you didn't. You just cowered in the corner and cried like a pussy. So I called you a stupid, useless cunt. And I left.

TERRY: No, you never called me that. You would never call me that. You love me.

JENNIFER: Yes, I did. That's what I called you. A stupid, useless cunt. And I would say it again. Because that's what you're acting like.

TERRY: No, why are you saying that? You love me. I thought you love me.

JENNIFER: If you're writing about us Terry, if you're documenting "us," our "love," at least have the balls to write the fuckin' truth.

JENNIFER exits.

TERRY starts crying. Still sobbing, he takes the box out from under the bed, opens it, takes out the gun, loads it, walks around with it a bit as he wipes his tears, clearly very distraught and dangerous. For a moment, he looks at the audience, gun in both hands, desperate and menacing, but he retreats. He then finds his usual meditative position with the gun under his chin and calms himself down.

BLACKOUT

End of Act Two

Act Three

25

ONSCREEN

INTERVIEW WITH POLICE SERGEANT –
THIS YEAR

JOURNALIST: Sergeant, you were the first
officer to arrive on the scene of the *Quasar Love*
tragedy, were you not?

SERGEANT: Yes, true, I was the first one in.
We responded to the emergency call and we had
been informed that a shooting was in progress,
but once we got there, it was all silent. The ordeal
was already over.

JOURNALIST: Would you mind explaining to
us what you found?

SERGEANT: It was one of the strangest
crime scenes I have ever walked into. There was
the tragic element of course, we found four dead
audience members, still in their seats, and at first
we thought that the shooter, or shooters, because
there were conflicting reports about who was
doing the shooting, might still be at large, so only

once we arrived onstage did we find the bodies of Terence and Jennifer, with the weapon still between them.

JOURNALIST: What was so strange about the scene though?

SERGEANT: It was them, I had never seen anyone die like that. We are still not exactly sure of how they did it but our theory always was that it must have been a simultaneous double suicide of sorts. We found them both naked, lying on the floor, on their sides, their lower bodies still interlocking, and the shotgun still right in between them. Their death was caused by a fatal wound to their heads coming from below, so both of them were missing their lower jaw and most of their face. What we conjectured was that they might have been kissing each other on top of the shotgun when they pulled the trigger, killing themselves instantly with the same shot.

CUT TO

INTERVIEW WITH PERFORMERS RESTAGING
QUASAR LOVE – THIS YEAR

JOURNALIST: Why *Quasar Love*? Out of all the performances out there why have you decided to restage this one?

ACTOR: The material has been begging our attention for years. We were always aware of the tragedy, yet it had also been a bit of a mystery, since nothing was recorded and there was never any real script. Then the notebooks of Terence Williams appeared online and it was only a matter of time before someone would actually try to restage *Quasar Love*. We thought it should be us.

JOURNALIST: But to what end? Is this just an occasion to "shock"?

ACTRESS: Well, first of all, we don't see what's wrong with "shocking" people. "Shock" has been undervalued and almost stigmatised by British and American critics that have aimed to keep theatre a middle-class, status-quo-preserving activity for decades. They turned the word "shocking" into an insult, a cheapening judgement, whereas it actually takes a lot of work to move an audience enough to achieve anything close to "shock." But, "shock" apart, we also wish to share a more honest understanding of who Jennifer and Terence were through this restaging of the notebooks. Since not much was ever known about the two lovers, and they have been demonized quite vehemently by the media after the tragedy, we believe they deserve another chance at getting their voices heard. If you read the original writing, it should become clearer that to simply label Jennifer and Terence as "homicidal maniacs" or "criminally insane" or "terrorists," is not enough of an explanation for their deeds.

JOURNALIST: So how *would* you explain their deeds then?

ACTRESS: I think that everything they did was a result of this toxic combination of alienation, abuse and desire. In a society driven by celebrity figures and popularity contests, there is nothing to hold back such a toxic relationship from spiralling out of control. Though today we are apprehensive of religious and conservative communities, in less liberalized systems there's a logic, flawed as it may be, but useful nonetheless, a formula that gives meaning to the suffering in our lives. Yet for people that live outside such communities, beyond conservative moral codes, in a world that constantly promotes only success, fame and fortune mixed in with this idealization of romantic love and unbridled sexuality, the suffering caused by a failure to achieve any form of satisfaction could become extremely dangerous. Both Jennifer and Terence harboured much resentment against the world for how they felt life had treated them and for how corrupt and disingenuous the world is, yet, beyond all the hate, their tragic act was clearly still a product of an intense desire to achieve an almost impossible togetherness that is recognized, respected and rewarded by the world around them, and isn't that what we all want?

JOURNALIST: But this sounds like you might be romanticizing their heinous act. Saying that what they did was a product of a misguided desire, could be insulting to those that died, and their families.

ACTOR: There is that risk, though it is not our intention. We live in a society where death is almost an evil rather than a natural reality, and murder of any sort is perceived as being absolutely morally unacceptable, even though our governments keep creating wars and sending citizens off to kill every single day. However, have we ever truly stopped to ask whether certain extreme human experiences and expressions that involve suffering, death and even murder may still be, in some way or another, poetically meaningful, maybe even necessary, for the full exploration and understanding of our life?

ACTRESS: The loss of life in itself is of course still not justified. No one is saying it was good that Jennifer and Terence killed those people. What we're saying is that whether what they did was morally reprehensible or not doesn't eliminate the fact that there might have been great poetry and art in what they did. Entire cultures, religions and belief systems have been erected on the poetic significance of immense suffering and unjust murder. Look at Jesus for example. The whole Christian civilization is rooted in the brutal performance of an undeserved execution, yet we may celebrate the poetry in that because we are distanced from the original deeds by time and geography. Finding poetry and beauty in tragedy has been a human reaction to our own mortality since the beginning of our species. We simply want to continue practicing this very human appreciation of death and tragedy through the passionate eyes of Jennifer Cole and Terence F. Williams.

FADE TO BLACK

27

Throughout this scene, there's a giant projection of JENNIFER's face. As the scene advances, the face deteriorates and pieces fall off until the whole face disintegrates and there is only a black hole left.

TERRY: The truth. She's asking for the truth. It's not enough to write. It's not enough to read. There's more, she says.

Why am I in here? Why don't I just open the door and leave? Why am I so afraid of going out there?

I think it's their faces, all of their faces, all those people. They've all been looking at me so weirdly for so long. And in here I only see hers, her face, I love that face. There's nothing I wouldn't do for that face.

Except fuck her. Why can't I fuck her?

Isn't that what a real man would do? I was never a real man. I could never compete in their games, attract attention without humiliation. I could never win. Why is winning so important? Why do we have to win all the time? And for a man, the ultimate prize for winning was always this, a woman's warm crotch. You win, so you fuck. But I could never win and I could never fuck and instead I want to be gentle and loving. I just want to love her. That's all. Not win her, not fuck her, just love her.

But what does that really mean? I want to keep her close, see her happy, maybe even feel happy, beside her.

Hold her. But I can't hold her. I want to so much but then she'd want to kiss me. If I hold her and hug her, she'll want to kiss me and touch me and take my clothes off.

Is that it? Is that love? Why? Why do I love her so much? Is it because she took me in and gave me shelter and listened to my stories and read my words?

Nobody else ever did. Nobody else ever read my writing. She read it and said it was amazing. Said it inspired her. She said the only reason why nobody has ever read it and loved it before is because the world is a sad, cruel and fucked-up place.

But then she keeps leaving. Coming and going. Seeing other people, doing other things, things I don't know of. I miss her. Every time she leaves with no explanation, I miss her and I want her back and I feel tortured.

Yet the second she comes back she terrifies me and all I want is to see her gone. Is this love?

She hurts me. She makes me suffer. It must be love. I hate myself. I hate myself for loving her. I hate myself because I love her.

Because she's my death. I know it. I can feel it. And I hate myself for not running away from it, for not walking to the door, opening it and leaving.

I'm the debris, the crushed and broken space dust falling in the gravitational pull of that gargantuan wound in space and time. I'm approaching the event horizon and I can see the entire universe right ahead of me, right within my grasp.

And the universe is beautiful because I'm not in it. The universe has distanced itself from me and I can see it in its entirety, the entire universe, without me in it, slipping beyond me.

And now all that is left is me. All I can see is me. The universe has slipped into the hole and as light warps itself around me, I can see myself slip into the hole following the entire universe. As every beam of remaining light is pulled from me into the black, I can see the back of my head right in front of my eyes.

And the back of my head is nothing but bloody bone, and pulverized brain; a hole inside a hole.

BLACKOUT

28

JENNIFER is now onstage writing in a notebook as she speaks. TERRY is reading a notebook in silence.

JENNIFER: I roam, Terry, that's what I do when I'm not at home. I roam the streets and meet strangers. Where do you think I get my money from?

Charity? I roam the streets, meet strangers and fuck. I fuck. I need to fuck.

Do I miss you? Of course I miss you. I miss your simplicity. I miss how you sometimes raise your head from your notebook and smile at me. I miss your body inside of me.

Is that possible? Can I miss something that never happened?

Maybe I can. Maybe I have had so many men inside of me that I can imagine you inside of me and miss you for not being there.

When will I come back? I'll come back when the pain of your rejection has subsided. You say I hurt you, Terry. I torture you. How do you think I feel every time I approach you and you cower in the corner of the room as if I were some demonic wraith?

Every time I'm rejected by you, I need ten other men to fill the wounds you leave inside of me.

What else do you want to know Terry?

Am I happy? No. I'm not. I haven't been in a very long while and you're delusional if you think you can make me happy.

I will never be happy Terry. Ever. Happiness is just something else for me not to believe in.

JENNIFER becomes motionless.

29

TERRY speaks.

TERRY:		There are new words… There are new words! In my notebooks. I'm finding new words. She brought the notebooks back the last time she left.

I'm sure she did it on purpose, I'm sure she left them all behind on purpose. She knew I'd read them again. She knew I'd find the new words, her words. Everywhere; in the margins, in between the lines, on my blank pages. Comments, remarks, jokes. Answers.

She's answered my questions.

I don't know whether to keep reading or not.
Could it be that knowing is actually worse than
not knowing?

I am so used to reading my own words I
sometimes forget that it is possible to read the
words of others.

TERRY becomes motionless.

30

JENNIFER speaks.

JENNIFER: Do you have any idea how much this
world disgusts me Terry? Why have we, I mean
us, human beings, the human fuckin' race, why
have we created such horrible civilisations? We're
nothing but a cancer, a sickening cancer, growing
on this planet, killing it whilst holding ourselves
prisoners with our civilised projects, political
systems and bureaucratic organisations.

Rats! Rotting rats in cages that eat and shit and fuck
and rear baby rats to grow and eat and shit and
fuck some more.

You know how many things could drive me over the edge? You know how many instances make me want to shoot my brains out?

Another bill to pay. Or another application to fill. Or another dotted line to sign. Or another law to obey. Or another something else they'll make me fuckin' buy!

Any of these, any single one of these and more, so many more obvious little things of this so-called pathetic civilised life can make me blow my fuckin' brains out, Terry.

When will you save me? What are you waiting for? (*She screams these last two questions in TERRY's unmoving face.*)

BLACKOUT

31

TERRY is still reading, not moving. JENNIFER is animated, writing and speaking out loud.

JENNIFER: Sometimes I offer extreme services. I tell people I can do things nobody else would subject themselves to. But like everything else in my life, I sometimes fail in that too.

I have just been with a man that wanted me to drink from a cup of a week's cum. He said he had been collecting it for me, masturbating and ejaculating in the cup as many times as he could each day and keeping it in the fridge so that when it's full enough he could call a girl like me and pay her to see her drink it.

I couldn't do it. He offered me good money, and offered me more when I refused to do it, he would have given me everything he owned to see me do it, but I just couldn't. I grabbed the cup and smashed it against the wall of his bedroom and ran out of his apartment in terror.

If he caught me, he would have killed me. I know it. He would have surely killed me.

Another man wanted me to shit on his chest and slide in it up and down as I jerked him off. I tried it. I thought what the fuck, it's my shit on his chest not the other way round. It was okay at first, almost kind of funny, but then as soon as I sat on him and started slipping in shit, I gagged and lurched on the man.

To my horror, he laughed and came even harder as the contents of my stomach hit his erect penis.

That day I made enough money for us to live on for two months in a single hour. It was the highest amount of money anybody had ever paid me for anything I had ever done in my entire life.

BLACKOUT

32

TERRY is still reading, not moving. JENNIFER is still the one speaking.

JENNIFER: I love the theatre. I do. And I have always wanted to have a proper career but nobody, literally nobody, has ever taken me seriously. You know how many auditions I've been to? How many projects I've tried to put together?

But as soon as they hear what I have to say, what I want to do, they just look at me in disgust and run away.

Constant humiliation and disappointment for years on end. There's literally no place in this world for me.

An entire childhood being told that if we work hard enough and if we want something hard enough we can be anything in life. Work hard and we will succeed. We will be rich and famous. Yeah, fuckin' right. As soon as you're of age to actually try something out they'll just change their tune.

It's not for everybody. Not everybody can make it. It's luck, dear. Find a job. You have to settle down. I will never settle down. I'll keep trying, I said. I won't give up, I said.

But no matter how hard I try, I always end up with a cock in my mouth and more self-hate. Because I am mediocre.

I hate myself, Terry. I hate myself deep and hard. Maybe that's why I love you. I love you because I hate myself. You are my perfect punishment. You are the good man, the kind one, the only one that could in some way love me like nobody else and yet I want to break you and make you fuck me exactly like everybody else. Because only if you fuck me like everybody else can I derive some splinter of satisfaction, a shred of pleasure in this damned body.

But as soon as you do that you, won't be yourself anymore. You won't be the broken Terry I love anymore. The day you fuck me you'll become a strong man just like the rest of them so I won't love you anymore.

And so I keep trying and I keep failing and I keep hating myself for having tried and failed. I hate myself for not getting you to fuck me, knowing that I will hate myself even more if I did. So I have to keep coming back for more failure, just to see which hate will kill me first.

JENNIFER becomes motionless.

33

TERRY speaks.

TERRY: She's asking me to save her. But all I can think of is killing her. She says she wants me to fuck her. She says I punish her every time I don't.

And yet she loves me for not fucking her. She knows that not fucking her is the only way I can love her. And even if I could fuck her, I will never risk losing her love, and yet all I do is push her away.

The only way out of this torment is death. Death is the only culmination possible for our love. Death is the only way I can save her and maybe end the pain, end the suffering.

But how?

I'm sorry Jennifer. I'm sorry I'm your punishment. I'm sorry I'm your pain. I'm sorry I love you. I don't think I can kill you, Jennifer.

TERRY stops moving again.

34

JENNIFER continues.

JENNIFER: What did they do to you Terry? What did they do to me?

Both of us were made to see things and feel things we might have never chosen to see or feel if we had ever been truly free to choose. Every time your brother made you look at what other men did, every time the world told you what it means to be a bloke and how to act like one and talk like one. Every time you were rejected and found wanting for not being like they wished, for not reaching their fuckin' standards.

I wasn't raped by my daddy or my uncle. My mother didn't pimp me out. My childhood was not some fucked-up, lower-class underdog story I can blame for becoming a whore and a failure. My childhood was simply the epitome of middle-class boredom. Not poor enough to be an excuse and not rich enough to be exciting. All I had to do was look around me and see all the lovely rich girls at school talk about the boyfriends I didn't have, and the trips I wasn't going on, or hear the crude working-class sluts talk about the cocks I wasn't putting in my mouth and the ass I wasn't showing on Saturday night. There I was, all alone, completely grey and unredeemable in every fuckin' way.

I saw women everywhere I looked around, women that walked like women, talked like women and did everything that women do. And I just couldn't do it. Whenever I tried, I tried too hard and I went too far, and they all saw right through me.

All I wanted was to succeed. I remember everyone telling me how bright I was, how intelligent I was, what a marvellous future I had ahead of me. Until the day I started disappointing everyone with every choice I made. Until they realized I do not fit in the box they had ready for me and so all they wanted to do was throw me out.

We are born. Then we are deformed and maimed. And then we are obliged to be successful. We are given impossible dreams only so that we can be broken and put in our place when we don't achieve them.

But I refuse. I refuse to be put in my place. I refuse to be another one of the million unknown faces of employable mediocrity. Help me, Terry. Help me show them. Together. We'll save each other; you'll save me, and I'll save you.

We'll use the gift, the gift in the box.

We should take it with us, Terry. We should go onstage and take it with us and do it there.

Can you imagine? Can you imagine their faces? Their horror as they see us unloading it onto them?

We'll create a moment in history they'll never forget. We'll become one on that stage like nobody ever has. Maybe you're right. Maybe your body is not enough. And my body will never be quenched. Our love won't submit itself to a fuck. To a pathetic bodily function. We can't close the holes inside our beings with some sweaty biological exercise that's only a few measures away from the pleasures of eating and defecating.

We need something else and maybe we have found it.

We hold it, together, between us, it will make us one in ways no love ever can, and we'll show them. We'll show them what it means to become something else altogether, something unforgettable.

JENNIFER pauses, motionless, and TERRY speaks.

TERRY: Could that be our answer? The metal? The spark? Is this why the box has been calling me and Jennifer? Is this how we transcend ourselves? Fire and blood? Light and darkness? Is this our quasar?

JENNIFER reacts to what TERRY has said.

JENNIFER: Maybe it's us, Terry, us together. We are
the quasar. The darkness and the light.
Destruction and Creation. Hate and Love. You
and I together, on that stage, creating a new world
as we destroy the old one. The world as we know
it, the world with us in it, the world with our
insignificant painful life writhing inside of it, will
be no more. We will bring that world to an end on
that stage. And after that, there will be a new
world, a world without us. A world where we
know only peace.

TERRY: I saw this already. I wrote this already.
The universe without us as it slips into the black
hole ahead of me. But it's not only me, it will be us,
both of us. The universe will slide down the
cosmic drain and there will be only us.

JENNIFER: We'll give this to them Terry. We'll go
there together, read them your words and show
them our truth; shoot our light from out of our
darkness and change their lives, rewrite their
whole universe.

Whoever answers our invitation, whoever dares
to come and judge us, whoever happens to have
been born under such a wretched star will be

blinded by the heat of our light, and will then remain forever enshrined in the cold of our darkness.

Next time I come, we'll go. We'll take it with us and we'll go, and we'll do it. I'm coming for you, Terence Williams. I'm coming back one last time, I'm taking you out of that wretched room and you will never have to see it again.

BLACKOUT

35

JENNIFER is gone. TERRY is alone once again. The box is in the middle of the room.

TERRY: I can hear her words loud and clear all around me. Every single word of her ultimate vision. I can see it all happening.

Me and her onstage and the thing in our hands. Both of us finding the meaning we've always longed for in a singular instant of light and destruction.

Is this what I have been waiting for all of my life? All of my life I have been writing and reading. Writing things and reading things I thought nobody will ever read or write. My life has so far been a very small and miserable bubble in space-time. A small and insignificant bubble that won't even leave a tremor once it pops out of existence.

But what if my bubble explodes with the power of a million stars? What if it creates waves and ripples that will shake the very fabric of time and space? Is it possible for my life not to be so insignificant? Can it truly be Jennifer to give me some meaning and relevance?

But I still don't think I can kill her. I can't kill you Jennifer. I can't kill you.

JENNIFER walks in through the door just in time to hear the last two sentences. This time she leaves the door ajar.

JENNIFER: You don't have to kill me, Terry. It won't be like that.

TERRY: Then how will we do it?

JENNIFER: Together. Together at the same time. One gesture. One action. And both of us are saved together.

TERRY: Maybe. Maybe yes, maybe I can do that, but the door…

JENNIFER: I will open it for you. I will open the door
              for you and help you out.

TERRY: Yes. With your help, I think I can do it
              with your help.

JENNIFER: Did you read it?

TERRY: Yes, everything.

JENNIFER: So? We can if you want to.

TERRY: Today?

JENNIFER: Yes, it's today. I have a place and there'll
              be people waiting for us.

TERRY: Is this the only way?

JENNIFER: Can you imagine any other way?

TERRY: No, I can't. But those people. We will
              destroy them.

JENNIFER: We'll give some of them rest, real peace
              and we will change others forever. Our act will
              make them reconsider everything.

TERRY: Oh my God. This is big. I don't know.
              What if we're sick, Jennifer? Maybe...maybe we

need to talk to somebody, maybe we need a
doctor.

JENNIFER: A doctor will not change the world for
us. You know what doctors do? They chop our
minds up with their drugs so we may take the
sordid shape of this world. They will make us fit
in! That's what they do. I don't want to fit it!

TERRY: But maybe if we fit in, we'll find some
kind of…who knows…inner peace?

JENNIFER: FUCK INNER PEACE! Inner peace is
what helps losers accept the fact that they are
losers. Inner peace is what this world wields to
hold us down in our little boxes when our dreams
become too much. Inner peace is what rich and
famous people sell us to siphon off the little we
have left. And I ain't buying that shit. No. Fuck
inner peace, Terry. We deserve way more than
that. We deserve a better world than this one, a
world where our love means something real and
everyone knows who we are and what we do.
We are entitled to it.

TERRY: But what if we deserve nothing? And
                what if they don't deserve the pain we will be
                raining on them?

JENNIFER: This is not you talking, Terry. This is the
                world you were brought up in. The world that
                treated you like shit since the day you were born.
                The world that told you how everyone is better
                than you, and you deserve to suffer because
                you're not good enough. But the world is wrong.
                You deserve everything that's right: freedom,
                dignity, respect, recognition, comfort, love—
                simply because you were born. Since that very
                second, you have deserved it all. Just as much as
                they deserve the pain they'll get. Yes, as soon as
                they bought that ticket so they could sit and judge
                they stopped being innocent and they became a
                very real part of this disgusting world that has put
                us aside. So they do deserve everything that's
                coming for them. There are no innocent people in
                this world Terry, you just have to stop thinking
                about what we're doing as causing pain. We are
                not causing pain. We are rewriting the world
                around us. We are rewriting the lives of the people
                in front of us.

TERRY: We are writing a new plot for their story.

JENNIFER: Exactly. Theirs and ours. Don't you feel
                excited?

TERRY: I don't know what I feel. All I know is
                that somehow I can feel this happening, I can feel
                all of this already in motion, slipping, as if by its
                own accord, and I do not intend to stop it because
                it feels good. It feels good to love you, and, I think,
                that this is what it means to love you.

JENNIFER: I can't stop myself either. Sometimes I
                want to, but I can't stop, I've turned a corner and
                there's nowhere left to go back to.

TERRY: There is no return. We've slipped into it
                now, and there's no way back out. This must be
                what it feels like, this must be what they call Event
                Horizon.

*JENNIFER says the following lines whilst undressing. TERRY
follows her example and starts to undress too. When he hesitates,
she helps him until they are both fully naked.*

JENNIFER: We are there already, in front of all their
                faces, on that stage, and I am seeing it. The hole.
                Time falling through it. The universe warping
                around us. Their faces distorted as light itself tries

to escape its pull. We are stretching into the black distance, the tips of my toes already feel a million miles away from the rest of my body. Your face is peeling off into the unknown atom by atom, and all of the past, the present and the future are uncoiling themselves—oblivious to the screams and cries of the maimed and the wounded. All we have to do is let go.

TERRY opens the box, takes out the shotgun and loads it. JENNIFER helps him in silence. TERRY and JENNIFER point the shotgun at the audience.

The stage goes dark and is enveloped in projected stars. The naked couple stand at the centre of a cosmic swirl, pointing the shotgun together at the audience. As the black hole forms and spins, a high-pitched, tone reaches a peak.

A burst of white light and BOOM. The first gunshot. Deafening. A second of silence. Then we can hear screams and chaos. A stampede. Another gunshot—BOOM. As loud as the first. More people screaming. Then two consecutive shots, BOOM, BOOM. And silence.

The projection is no longer visible. A spot of light beams on TERRY and JENNIFER as they kneel down on the floor facing each other. They hold the shotgun together right in between them, pointing upwards, two hands steadying the barrel, the other two on the trigger. They kiss passionately with the shotgun under their chins.

This is the only time they kiss in the entire performance. They keep kissing as the light fades to black.

THE END